CZERNY
THIRTY NEW STUDIES
IN TECHNICS
Opus 849

Edited and Recorded by Matthew Edwards

To access companion recorded performances online, visit:
www.halleonard.com/mylibrary
Enter Code
5321-7654-6316-4367

On the cover:
Interior with Woman at the Piano
by Felix Edouard Vallotton
(1865–1925)
© Galerie Vallotton, Lausanne, Switzerland/The Bridgeman Art Library

ISBN 978-1-4584-1160-0

G. SCHIRMER, Inc.

DISTRIBUTED BY

HAL•LEONARD®
CORPORATION
7777 W. BLUEMOUND RD. P.O. BOX 13819 MILWAUKEE, WI 53213

www.musicsalesclassical.com
www.halleonard.com

CONTENTS

The price of this publication includes access to companion recorded performances online, for download or streaming, using the unique code found on the title page. Visit **www.halleonard.com/mylibrary** and enter the access code.

HISTORICAL NOTES

CARL CZERNY (1791–1857)

Although born into a rather humble family with few prospects of prosperity or good education, Carl Czerny is today a household name, well-known to pianists around the world. Through good fortune, and a degree of talent, he interacted with some of the most important names in both Classical and Romantic literature. The list of his contacts is nearly unbelievable: he studied with Beethoven and Clementi; taught Liszt, Thalberg, and Leschetizky; and associated with countless others including Chopin, Constanze Mozart (Mozart's wife), Franz Xaver Süssmayer (Mozart's pupil), Andreas Streicher (the piano manufacturer), and many more. He was the first—or at least one of the first—to perform many of Beethoven's works, and wrote original compositions of such popularity in his day, that publishers were willing to print anything he submitted. Very often, they did not even care to hear or see it before the contract was signed.

Without doubt, Czerny lived in interesting times, and was privileged to observe first-hand the transition from the Classicism of Haydn and Mozart to the passion of the Romantics. Of course, none other than Ludwig van Beethoven was his guide through this most significant progression. Czerny stood as an observer at the crossroads of these two styles, but he also saw—and, to a great degree, assisted in—the transformation of keyboard technique. By the combination of the fame of his publications, and his successful teaching career, he became one of the foremost authorities on piano playing during this time. Even today, his legacy is sustained by his multiple collections of exercises and pedagogical works. Though his life is primarily summarized by these, a thorough study would reveal a man of many skills and interests.

Czerny's grandfather had been a violinist, and his father, Wenzel Czerny (1750–1832), played several instruments, including piano, organ, and oboe. Wenzel did not marry until 1786, delayed by his fifteen years of service in the army.[1] Carl, who would be the couple's only child, was born in Vienna, Austria, on February 21, 1791. The family briefly moved to Poland, but returned to Vienna in 1795, where his father began a moderately successful career of piano teaching and piano maintenance.

It is no surprise, then, that Carl was attracted to the piano early on; his autobiography states that he began playing at the age of three, and by seven was also composing.[2] His parents kept him close to home, generally removed from most of his would-be playmates, providing ample opportunity for his musical interests. In addition, much of his education came from his father's piano students, who, as part of their lesson fees, tutored Carl in a variety of subjects including French, German, and literature. Yet about this relative isolation, he states that he "never missed the friendship of other boys, and never went out without my father."[3]

His father's skill as a pianist and teacher was at least good enough to give young Carl an excellent foundation in technique and sight-reading. He describes it thus:

> My father had no intention whatever of making a superficial virtuoso out of me; rather, he strove to develop my sight-reading ability through continuous study of new works and thus to develop my musicianship. When I was barely ten I was already able to play cleanly and fluently nearly everything by Mozart, Clementi, and the other piano composers of the time; owing to my excellent musical memory I mostly performed without the music. Whatever money my father could set aside from the scant pay for his lessons was spent on music for me…[4]

Perhaps the critical moment in the life of Carl Czerny was his introduction to Beethoven. One of Beethoven's closest friends was a man named Wenzel Krumpholz, who also happened to be a friend of the Czerny family. Through Krumpholz, Carl became aware of the great composer, and as soon as he was able, began playing as much of his music as he could find. Impressed by the 10-year old's pianism and musicality, Krumpholz agreed to take the boy and his father to Beethoven's home for a formal introduction.

The apartment was high above the street, and was rather unkempt and disheveled. Other musicians were there rehearsing, but they quickly became an impromptu audience for Carl as he sat down at Beethoven's piano to play. He performed the first movement of Mozart's C major piano concerto (K. 503), and Beethoven's own recently released Pathétique Sonata. When he finished, Beethoven uttered the words that quite possibly set Czerny's future success in motion: "The boy is talented, I myself want to teach him, and I accept him as my pupil. Let him come several times a week."[5]

Although the lessons lasted little more than a year due to Beethoven's growing need to focus on composition and the Czernys' financial situation, the relationship continued to grow until Beethoven's death in 1827. Czerny often worked closely with him, even writing the piano reduction for the publication of *Fidelio*. He also taught piano to Beethoven's nephew Carl, and gave widely successful early performances of Beethoven's works.

Performing never took a central role in Czerny's career—in fact, he cancelled his very first concert tour in 1805 even though it was supported by Beethoven himself![6] Instead, he turned his attention to teaching and composing, and found significant success in both areas. For many years, he taught twelve hours daily, and, by means of his prominent reputation, was able to charge very well for the instruction. While it was common for him to teach many of the most talented young people of the day, at least one eclipsed them all. Czerny describes the first meeting like this:

One morning in 1819... a man brought a small boy about eight years of age to me and asked me to let that little fellow play for me. He was a pale, delicate-looking child and while playing swayed on the chair as if drunk so that I often thought he would fall to the floor. Moreover, his playing was completely irregular, careless, and confused, and he had so little knowledge of correct fingering that he threw his fingers over the keyboard in an altogether arbitrary fashion. Nevertheless, I was amazed by the talent with which Nature had equipped him.[7]

Rarely does one hear such a dismal description of the great Franz Liszt, but such was Czerny's first impression. Over the next fourteen months, he worked with the boy every evening, requiring him to learn rapidly and work tirelessly on technical exercises including Czerny's own works.[8]

If we combine Czerny's published and unpublished works, his compositions number more than 1,000. He wrote symphonies, variations, arrangements, chamber works, and sacred choral works in addition to his numerous pedagogical works. Not all of his music was received well—in particular, Schumann's review of a piano work entitled *The Four Seasons* stated that "it would be hard to discover a greater bankruptcy in imagination than Czerny has proved."[9] Harsh, to be sure, but many of the greatest pianists, including Liszt and Chopin, played his works throughout the continent, to great acclaim. To this day, many of the sonatas are regularly performed.

Professionally, Czerny's reputation remained generally high throughout his life. Personally, however, he remained alone, never marrying. His brief autobiography, which describes his life to 1842, ends rather abruptly with the following sentence: "In 1827 I lost my mother and five years later (1832) my father, and was thus left all alone, since I have no relatives whatever."

Carl Czerny died on July 15, 1857. A humble beginning, a quiet passing; but in between, a remarkable life.

– Mathew Edwards

PERFORMANCE NOTES

Introduction to Czerny's Music

Czerny organized his compositions for piano into four categories:

- Studies and exercises
- Easy pieces for students
- Brilliant pieces for concerts
- Serious music[10]

He is best known for his pedagogical and technical works, yet he also wrote many compositional treatises. He seems to have held to the idea that performance and composition should go hand in hand, and even expressed disappointment that Liszt had not had sufficient instruction from him in composition.[11] He was a pedagogue at heart, and sought through all of his works to teach and admonish young musicians.

Thirty New Studies in Technics, Op. 849

These etudes could be described as an "intermediate" set, at least in comparison with Czerny's other technical works. Certainly they are generally more difficult than the works for younger students such as *The Little Pianist*, Op. 823 and *Practical Method for Beginners*, Op. 599. In a way then, this publication is a preparation for the more difficult etudes, such as *The School of Velocity*, Op. 299 and *The Art of Finger Dexterity*, Op. 740.

The publication does have a small degree of flow in terms of difficulty; i.e., a general movement from somewhat easier to somewhat more challenging. However, the progression is not nearly so obvious or so intentional as in his *Practical Method for Beginners*, Op. 599. The works here are written to be studies in certain kinds of technique, almost to be selected by the teacher on an "as-needed" basis for the challenges being faced by a particular student in other repertoire. This is, after all, how many of his etudes came into being, some even being written during his lessons! Rather than attempt to use these in a chronological way,

examine how they might apply to a students' other pieces.

In this publication, Czerny will often focus on a certain type of technique in several different etudes. It is very helpful to practice these groups of etudes together, thereby studing a single technique with several approaches. One example comes from numbers 12 and 26, studying repeated notes; in this case, the second etude practices the same concept, but in a slightly more difficult presentation. In the section on the individual pieces, I have mentioned several of the etudes that could be studied together in this manner.

General Suggestions

It is extremely important to remember that these works are not technical studies alone. There are two clear goals in these etudes:

- The practice and attainment of good physical and keyboard technique
- The practice and attainment of musical playing

While these goals may seem like two separate things, the reality is that they are inextricably linked. A scale played with an awkward finger crossing will never sound as smooth and even as one with a comfortable fingering; chords played with great tension will have a strong tendency to be harsh. Therefore, the physical approach must be planned in conjunction with the musical design.

Technique and Physical Approach

Overall, my approach to piano technique is one of relaxed arms and hands, rounded fingers supporting the weight of the arm, and freedom and economy of motion. In my frequent comments on technique (in the section on the individual pieces), I have attempted to clarify some of these approaches to the keyboard that have proven extremely useful to me and to my students. However, it is understandably difficult to convey the subtleties of piano technique in just a few words. At the very least, tension should be avoided, and careful attention should be paid to the physical study of *how* a passage is best and most naturally played.

As an example, many of the pieces in this publication focus on scales and arpeggios. It is typically a sign of a technical problem if there is an unexpected accent or rhythmic unevenness in a scale or arpeggio. It is most important, in order to overcome this problem, that the fingers and hand (and by extension, the entire body) stay relaxed; by tensing your muscles, everything becomes more difficult. Relaxed playing gives much more freedom to the movements of the hand and arm.

Tempos

Metronome indications in this edition are intentionally absent, in part to encourage the technical focus to be on the physical technique of playing. Unfortunately, with a metronome marking at the top of the page, the goal can often become only the achievement of that tempo, even at the expense of better technique. The tempos on the recording are merely examples, and are by no means the definitive speed. Remember that there may be many appropriate tempos for these etudes. Each student should play the faster pieces as quickly and as cleanly as good technique will allow.

Fingering

Remember that the fingerings given here are suggestions only. Every hand is different, so every fingering should be examined; don't try to force a fingering that may not work for you!

Generally, I have tried to follow a few principles for my fingering choices:

- A relaxed hand: In the majority of cases I have tried to keep the fingers close together, and the hand moving as a unit. This more easily allows the fingers to stay relaxed and the hand to move both faster and more smoothly. Of course, stretches are required when extending to the octave and beyond (or the sixth, for smaller hands), but allow the hand to move toward the extended note, keeping the fingers relaxed.

- Economy of motion: this applies to the fingers alone, as well as to the entire hand. Minimize the number of crossovers in a passage, grouping as many notes into one hand position as possible. Imagine, for example, if a simple C-major arpeggio over three octaves were played with only the first and second fingers; there would be several hand positions, creating a much more difficult passage.

Ornamentation

"The graces, namely, the shake, the turn, the appoggiatura, etc., are the flowers of music; and the clear, correct, and delicate execution of them, embellishes and exalts every melody and every passage. But, when they are played stiff, hard, or unintelligibly, they may rather be compared to blots of ink or spots of dirt."[12]

A great deal of research and opinion are available on this topic. While it is important to be familiar with the current conventional wisdom, one cannot forget the fundamental principle that ornaments, as Czerny himself said above, are decorative and improvisatory. They are decorative in the sense that they are subservient to the primary line, and improvisatory in that their execution varies— slightly or greatly—from performer to performer. In the Baroque era, J.S. Bach wrote a very detailed chart, explaining the ornamentation written in his works. Yet Sandra Rosenblum, in her extremely helpful book *Performance Practices in Classic Piano Music* states that "Neither Haydn, Mozart, nor Beethoven left any systematic instructions for the performance of ornaments."[13] Clementi is perhaps the most significant composer to write instructions on ornamentation, yet Rosenblum further states that "Although many treatises discussed ornaments and gave instructions for their performance, there was not—and is not now—complete agreement regarding either notation or performance."[14] The point to be seen here is that while there may be some general "rules" about the execution of turns, trills, and appoggiaturas, there are still many valid variables left to the unique and instinctive choice of each performer.

Notes on the Individual Exercises

No. 1: Allegro

This is an excellent introduction to these studies. The generally small range of the patterns in each measure will allow the focus to be on a rounded hand without the need to stretch for larger intervals. Let the fingers stay relaxed throughout. For the half and whole notes, hold these down with as little weight as possible; do not keep heavy pressure on them as this will actually cause more work for the other fingers.

No. 2: Allegro molto

The left hand is the technical focus here, and is once again in a rather close position for the majority of the piece. The accompanimental pattern is one of the more common in the Classical Era, so the exercise is extremely practical. The quarter notes in the left hand should not necessarily be held for their full value, as in many respects, the notation is used simply to clarify the bass line. Again, keep the fingers relaxed and light. Make sure the melody is clear and energetic, capturing the attention of the listener more than the accompaniment.

No. 3: Allegro non troppo
Be careful not to play the chords too heavily on each beat. A subtle dynamic direction will help them support the right hand and enhance the shape of the line. Keep the triplets light but prominent, making every effort to follow the two-bar phrases completely to their close.

No. 4: Allegro
This etude is an extension of number 3, using sixteenths instead of triplets. The right-hand melody is a bit more clearly defined by the quarter notes, but careful attention to dynamic shape is required to prevent the repeated notes from being too plain and flat. Assisting that shape is the more melodic left hand.

No. 5: Vivace giocoso
The left-hand triplet pattern from number 2 appears again in this etude in a slightly faster tempo. Keep the triplets light, so they do not become the focus of the listener's attention. The more challenging element of this etude is the right hand. Because of the speed of the thirty-second notes, it can be difficult to keep unwanted accents from breaking the line. Think of the thirty-second notes as simply "falling" out of the hand into the keyboard, and not being "pushed" or "snapped."

No. 6: Allegro leggiero
In the right-hand patterns that encompass a fifth, keep the hand as relaxed as possible. This is an excellent pattern for learning to play from the hand and arm, without tightening the fingers and grabbing the notes. In particular, the placement of the patterns can help prepare the student to be relaxed in the longer scale passages; maintain the same comfortable hand position for both. This exercise is well-suited as a preliminary study to number 11.

No. 7: Vivace
Again, the quarters found with the left-hand sixteenths seem to be for indicating the bass line rather than a suggestion to emphasize or even

to literally hold the note. By contrast, when this appears in the right hand, it does indeed seem more logical to hold the note so that the melody is legato as indicated by the phrase marking. When these notes are held (right or left hand), be sure not to maintain heavy pressure on the held note. Just enough to keep the key down—no more, no less—and the remaining notes will be more free, clear, and even. Pay close attention to the *dolce* marking beginning in measure 17; this section (through measure 24) provides a lovely contrast to the more energetic opening.

No. 8: Vivace
In this rapid exercise for scale passagework, one practice focus should be in eliminating any accent where finger crossing is required. Generally, I have tried to use the same C-major fingering for each octave passage unless absolutely necessary. One example of a change is in measure 17, where the nine-note passages require the thumb to cross under the fourth finger twice. As always, keep the fingers relaxed, merely allowing the weight of the arm to fall into the keyboard through the fingers.

No. 9: Allegretto vivace
This exercise is good to pair with number 8, as the scales are now in the left hand. They are slightly more complicated than the previous exercises, and typically involve more black notes. When first learning the work, practice slowly to maintain a comfortable hand position, particularly in the longer scales. Remember also to be as musical as possible with the hand that does not play scales.

No. 10: Allegro moderato
A very delicate and beautiful etude, this may prove more difficult than it first appears. In general, it should not sound as if two hands are playing—each note should flow directly to the next without an unwanted accent where the hands change. There are passages where one note does need to be more prominent to point out an interesting line. A clear example of this is in measures 9–12, where the left hand note leads in shaping the rising dynamic line. A second, and perhaps less obvious example, is in measures 13–14, where a slight emphasis on the changing right hand notes gives us a beautiful line to follow.

No. 11: Molto vivace
In some ways, this exercise is an extension of number 6; it may be a good idea to study these two together. The same relaxed playing of a five-note pattern encouraged by number 6 is

here stretched out to a full octave. With careful practice, the finger-crossing can feel just as free and without accent. The main difficulty will be to keep the third finger from tightening just before the thumb crosses. First practice the initial three notes of the scale patterns, staying relaxed when the third finger is played. When comfortable with that, add the remaining notes, and keep the hand moving upward for the entire scale. Finally, don't forget to give dynamic direction to the scales.

No. 12: Allegretto animato

Repeated notes are often a struggle for pianists, and can be a cause of great tension if played incorrectly. It is most important not to play these with tight and tense fingers, almost "clawing" at each group of notes. Rather, drop the fingers into the notes and allow the hand to move slightly forward, as if "following-through" after each finger plays. Notice that the dynamic indicated at the beginning is *piano*; striving to achieve this level will help in playing them correctly. Also, don't forget to be as musical as possible with the left hand.

No. 13: Molto vivace e leggiero

No matter how small the interval, each pair in the right hand should utilize a very free rotation, with a relaxed wrist. Often, students are told to "rotate the wrist," but it actually extends all the way back to the elbow; a simple examination of the movement away from the piano will show this to be true. Be very careful not to turn this simply into an exercise; there are some beautiful lines here, and appropriate shading can make it a very exciting piece. For the double notes in measures 45–47, rotate to the center of the interval— rotating to the top or bottom note will result in the other note likely being missed, or not heard at all.

No. 14: Molto vivace

The right hand is in constant motion in this etude. Five-note patterns, scales, and Alberti-like figures from previous etudes all combine in this one piece. Shape the thirty-second notes as a melodic line especially when the left hand has staccato chords. In measures 9–16, however, the left hand can lead melodically while the right-hand figures sound a bit more like accompaniment. Be very careful to keep the third, fourth, and fifth fingers relaxed here, as they will have a strong tendency to tighten up during this repetitive movement.

No. 15: Allegretto vivace

Finally getting away from scale technique, this work focuses on arpeggios in both hands. The hand should have a good arched or rounded shape whether the arpeggio is spread over a single octave or over four octaves. If the hand is flat, and lying close to the keys, the fingers will have to work much harder, and the crossovers will likely be uneven.

Keep the hand in motion as the arpeggios move up and down the keyboard; staying in position until the last moment before a crossover will actually make the arpeggio more difficult. Also, make sure that the elbow does not swing out away from the body when crossing as this will cause the wrist to twist more than it should. In particular, be careful of this in measures 27–33 where many of the arpeggios begin on the second finger.

I have put in a few slightly unconventional fingerings, at least by the standard of common arpeggio playing. As always, printed fingerings are not the law, but may be worth at least a try.

No. 16: Molto vivace energico

This work has some small similarities to the opening of Liszt's eighth Transcendental Etude, "Wilde Jagd." Here we see the five-note pattern again, but it leaps around the keyboard, rather than remaining stationary. Interspersed between these patterns are chords in both hands. It is not uncommon for the last few notes of the pattern, or the second of the two chords, to be accented, tense, or rushed. Usually, this happens because the performer is worrying too much about what comes *after* the figure they are currently playing. In the eagerness to make a successful leap, the last notes (or chord) serve(s) as a "jumping-off point," resulting in accents, or notes clumped together. The answer can be stated: be where you are. In other words, don't be concerned about beat 3 while you are still playing beat 2. It takes time to learn this kind of patience, but when the hand and arm truly move freely, they can move with great speed and accuracy.

No. 17: Vivace giocoso

Ornaments in Classical and Romantic music are a source of great controversy. Perhaps the only rule from these eras without exception is: "All rules of ornamentation have exceptions." Predominantly, the research shows that there are many situations in which the performer can choose the manner of execution based upon the context of the ornament, and to a degree, on personal preference. I have chosen, on this recording, to play the ornaments of measure 1 on the beat. Playing them before the beat requires faster execution, and creates a more abrupt rhythm; simply put, I prefer the more lyrical sound of these ornaments on the beat.

Another issue to be considered is the turn indication seen first in measure 25. Many editions use this marking, while just as many continue with the ornament used in measure 1.

One generalization about ornaments of this era is that they should always enhance, or contribute to the line. If they are played loudly, suddenly, out of context, or out of control, they will be more of a distraction than anything.

No. 18: Allegro risoluto
At first glance, this may appear to be just another scale etude, but Czerny introduces a few measures of trill work, and scales in parallel sixths. The trills require special attention, as they are "anchored" by a lower half note. Hold this note with minimal pressure and allow the upper notes in the trill to rotate freely. For the parallel sixths, listen very carefully for a smooth and even line. Try to feel as though both hands and arms are moving together as one; often, awareness of the synchronization of these two body parts will help the fingers to play smoothly together as well.

No. 19: Allegro scherzando
Although they are not notated as ornaments, the right hand thirty-second notes should be played just as gracefully. Be sure that both fingers are completely relaxed and fall gently into the keys. If the fingers tense before playing each pair, then they will be too accented, and it will be very difficult to control any kind of dynamic line. Make sure the piece always feels as if it is in a large 2-beat meter; i.e., the first measure is beat 1, the second measure is beat 2. This will add to the light and almost bouncing character of the work.

No. 20: Allegro piacevole
Perhaps taking its cue from the triplet writing at the end of number 19, this etude extends those ideas to the entire piece. It should have a similar light and graceful quality. Take care to make the line as long as possible; certainly don't accent the first of each triplet. Also, the left hand provides great contrast with its staccato chords; practice this hand alone to hear how the accompaniment supports and even occasionally leads the right. Let it be especially melodic in measures 17–20.

No. 21: Allegro vivo
The chromaticism of this work puts the fingers closer together than in previous works; however, they can still be played in the same relaxed manner. Especially in the longer passages, keep the hand well over the white and black notes. If the hand stays low and close to the white notes, the rhythm will be prone to unevenness.

No. 22: Allegro
Short and long trills are studied in this work, predominantly for the right hand. It is important to remember to rotate from finger to finger, even in these small intervals. As you change to another pair of fingers, be sure to change the center of balance so the rotation remains constant and even. The same rotation can be utilized when a finger is crossed over the thumb, as in measure 1.

Measures 16–19 may prove particularly difficult. As suggested for earlier studies, hold the half notes gently so that the upper notes can rotate freely. Work carefully to make a nice melodic line with the half notes.

No. 23: Allegro comodo
This etude extends parallel playing beyond the octave to parallel thirds, sixths, and tenths. Listen closely as you play the scales to make sure each hand plays exactly together. The piece is particularly effective if the hands rise and fall exactly together dynamically.

No. 24: Allegro moderato
This is another etude that may look easier than it actually is, yet it can be an extremely helpful exercise for a very common technique. Evenness is critical here. Focus primarily on the left hand, as the "leader" of the rhythm. With the left hand solidly in place rhythmically, the right will more easily fall into the correct place between the beats. The natural tendency may be to focus on the right hand, but in reality, it is far more difficult to be even. The most difficult section in the piece may be measures 17–22, where the left hand is more accompanimental and the right is clearly the melody. Again, focus on the left hand to lead the rhythm. Emphasize the contrasts of articulation throughout.

No. 25: Allegro en galop
With so many broken chords and arpeggios in this etude, special care must be taken to make it as musical as possible. Often this will involve looking for individual notes to emphasize in order to give the illusion of a melodic line. An example from

the recording is measures 12–15; a slight emphasis on certain notes turns this otherwise technical passage into a beautiful, lyric moment. Also, give a subtle emphasis to the upper note of the left hand chords to enhance the overall lyrical quality of this piece.

Keep the hand rounded throughout and avoid stretching the fifth finger out to reach the higher notes—move the entire hand, not just the finger. For the passages where the second finger crosses over, remember to keep the elbow relaxed and move the hand forward to place the finger in the best position to play the note.

No. 26: Allegretto vivace

In some ways, the repeated notes here are more difficult than those in number 12 in that there tend to be four at a time, instead of three, and they combine with other notes to make up a lyrical melody. If a comfortable and relaxed approach was achieved in number 12, then this will be a natural extension of the same techniques. Phrase markings are drawn over many of the repeated notes, so they must sound as if they are part of the melody and not just a fast rhythmic "introduction" to the phrase.

Voice the left-hand upper notes in measures 9–16 being careful to follow each long phrase all the way to the end. In measures 17–21 and 29–32 the focus should be the subtle movements in the harmonic progression.

No. 27: Allegro comodo

The most critical technique necessary for this piece is the ability to move the arm quickly over distances of nearly three octaves without crashing into the notes once the move is complete. For practice, choose any two notes on the keyboard that are about four octaves apart. Next, with the third finger, try to play those two notes from lowest to highest as quickly as possible. Initially, do not worry too much about playing the upper note accurately; focus on the freedom of the arm movement. The more tension that is used in traveling the distance, the greater the chance that the upper note will be too loud, and/or out of control. Notice that as the arm is relaxed, the speed increases, as does the accuracy. This is the kind of control required for this etude.

Be as lyrical as possible for the brief motives with phrase markings. Also, occasionally practice the melodic notes without the Alberti motion;

the rests between notes require you to sing the melody in your mind, so the line is longer, and the short notes sound like part of the melody, rather than the accompaniment.

No. 28: Allegro

The wrist must, of course, be supple and flexible for this piece in order to play each of the chords clearly and distinctly. However, just as important is to be relaxed in the elbow and shoulder. Any tension or tightness in any one of these three locations will turn this etude into a very difficult and even painful piece. To see the effect of this, try (only once!) to play the repeated notes with a relaxed wrist, but a locked elbow and shoulder. The wrist will tire quickly, and the importance of this point will be obvious.

Be particularly careful with the left hand beginning at measure 9; as always, hold the lower note lightly once it has been played, which will make it possible to keep the wrist relaxed for the repeated notes.

No. 29: Allegro molto

Like number 10, this should nearly sound as if a single hand is playing the entire piece. The two main items to focus on are the smoothness of the transition between the hands and the consistency of the rhythm and the line as the hands change. Be sure not to let the hands crash into each other or crowd each other out. Indeed, your hands may find themselves in a few awkward positions but never allow that to create tension; keep the hands rounded, relaxed, and well above the keys.

No. 30: Molto vivace

A study in even, unison playing, this etude should not be seen as simply a return to the first half of the publication. Shape the line as if the entire piece were one long melody so that it doesn't become a "scale etude."

Notes:

[1] Little is known about his mother—she is described by Czerny simply as "a Moravian girl."

[2] Czerny, Carl. "Recollections from My Life." Trans. Ernest Sanders. *The Musical Quarterly*, Vol. 42, No. 3. (Jul., 1956), p. 303.

[3] ibid., 305.

[4] ibid., 303.

[5] ibid., 307.

[6] Stephan D. Lindeman and George Barth, "Czerny, Carl," *Grove Music Online*, ed. Laura Macy: www.grovemusic.com (accessed 1 Feb. 2011).

[7] Czerny, Carl. "Recollections from My Life." Trans. Ernest Sanders. *The Musical Quarterly*, Vol. 42, No. 3. (Jul., 1956), pp. 314–315.

[8] Alan Walker, et al, "Liszt, Franz." *Grove Music Online*, ed. Laura Macy: www.grovemusic.com (accessed 1 Feb. 2011).

[9] Stephan D. Lindeman and George Barth, "Czerny, Carl," *Grove Music Online*, ed. Laura Macy: www.grovemusic.com (accessed 1 Feb. 2011).

[10] ibid.

[11] Czerny, Carl. "Recollections from My Life." Trans. Ernest Sanders. *The Musical Quarterly*, Vol. 42, No. 3. (Jul., 1956), p. 316.

[12] Czerny, Carl. *Letters to a Young Lady, on the Art of Playing the Pianoforte*. Trans. J. A. Hamilton. (Da Capo Press: New York), 1982.

[13] Rosenblum, Sandra. *Performance Practices in Classic Piano Music* (Indiana University Press: Bloomington, 1988), p. 216.

[14] ibid., p. 217.

THIRTY NEW STUDIES IN TECHNICS Opus 849

Thirty New Studies in Technics

Carl Czerny
Op. 849

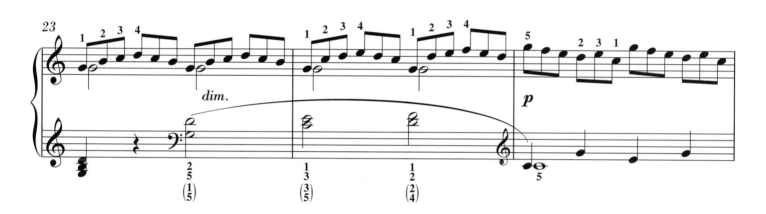

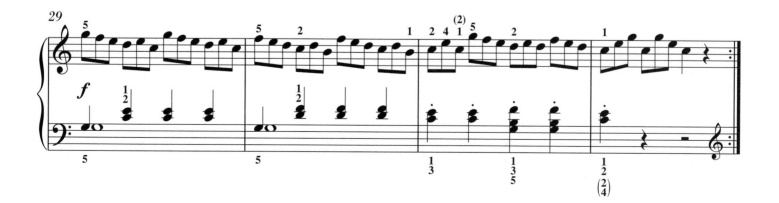

Allegro molto

2.

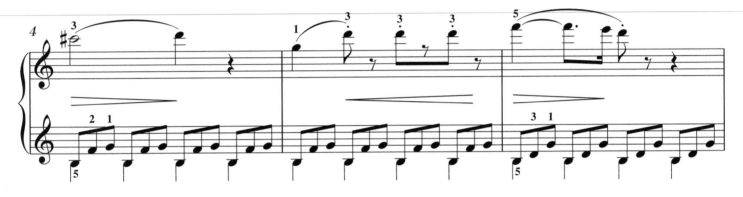

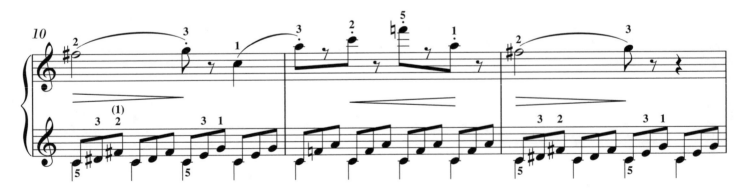

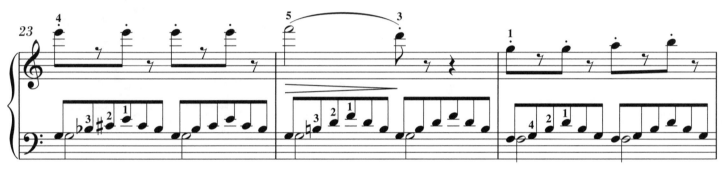

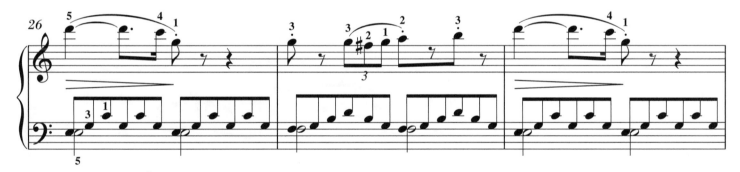

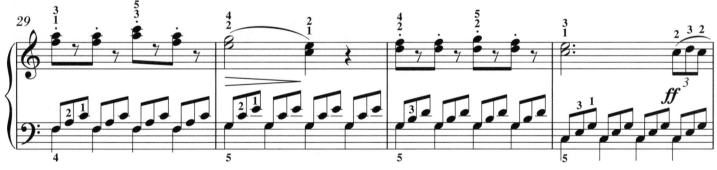

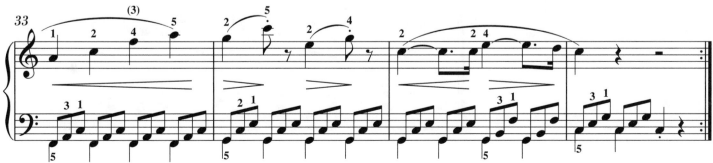

Allegro non troppo

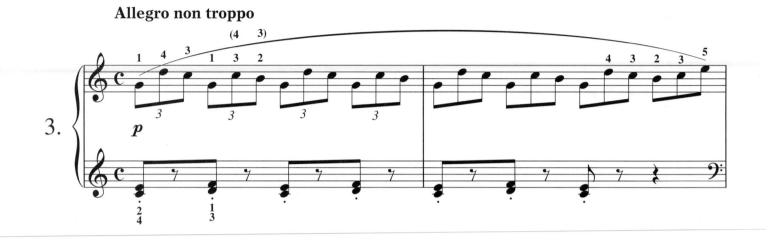

3.

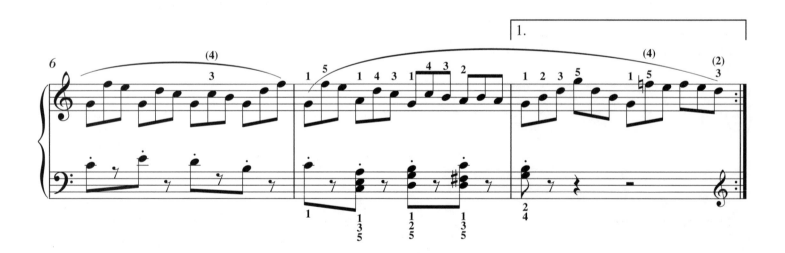

1.

2.

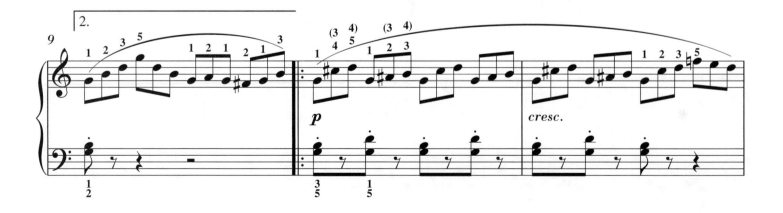

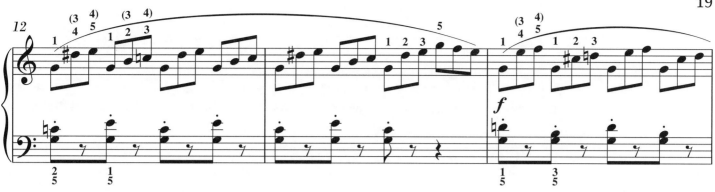

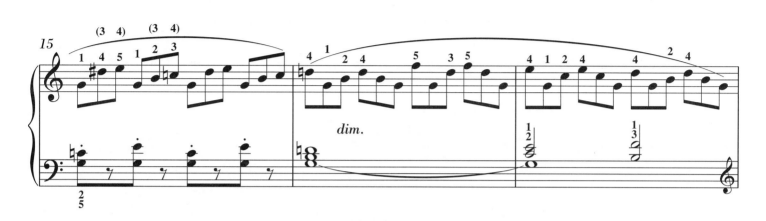

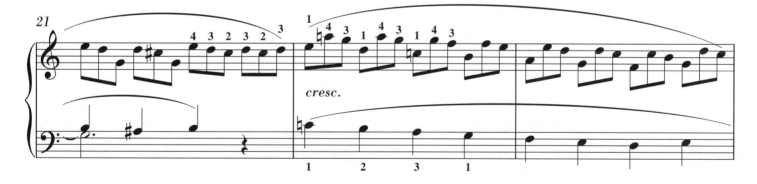

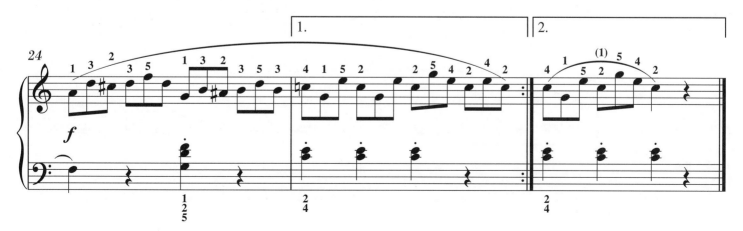

Allegro

4.

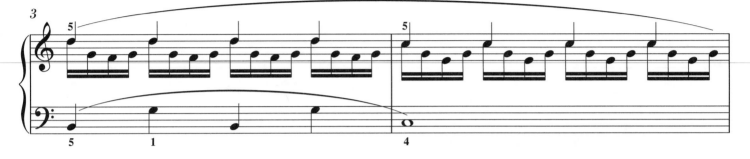

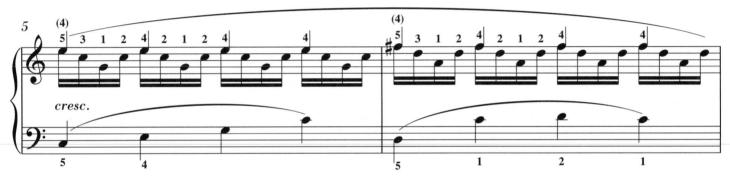

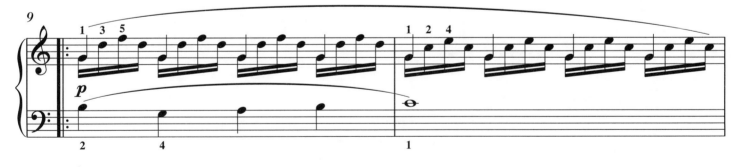

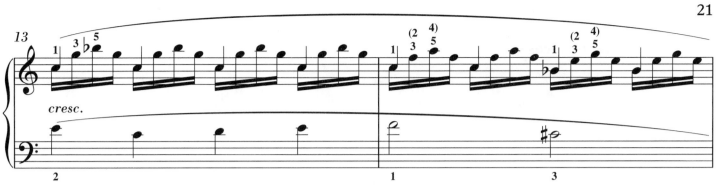

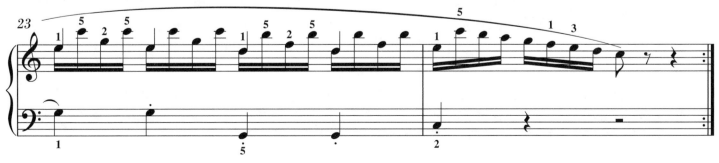

Vivace giocoso

5.

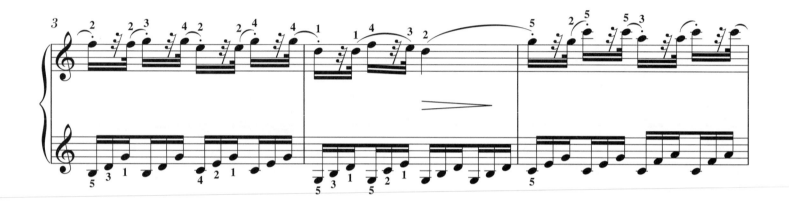

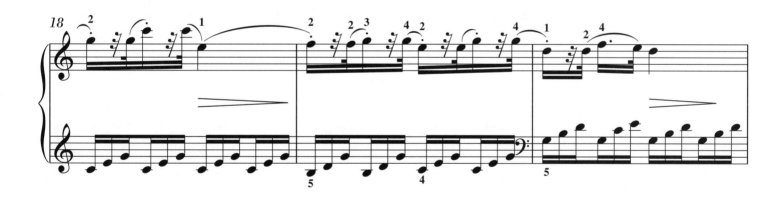

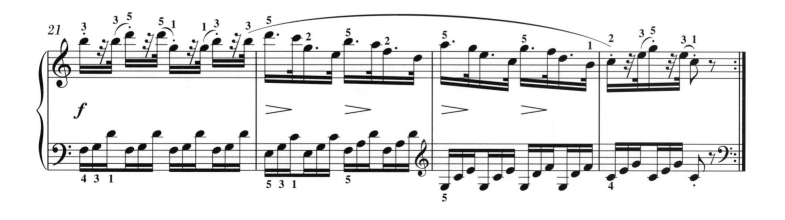

Allegro leggiero

6.

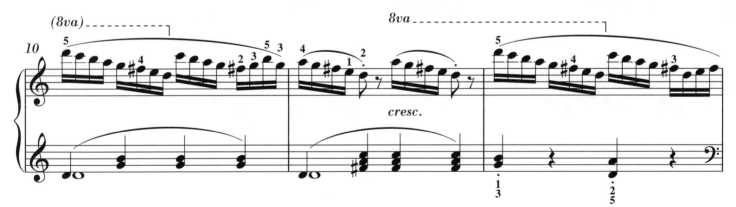

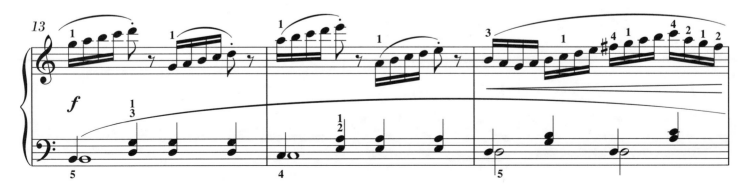

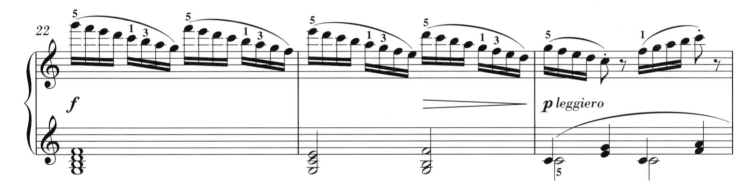

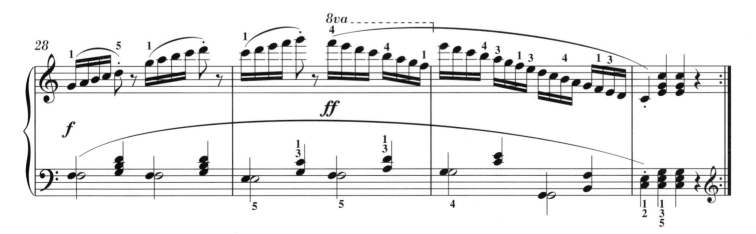

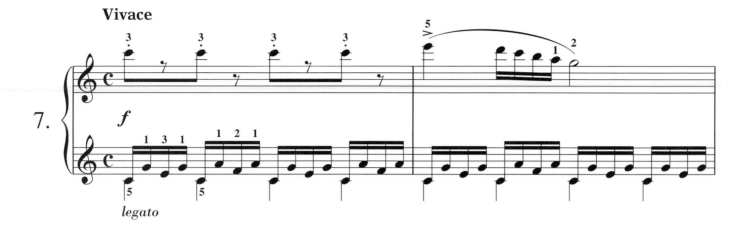

7.

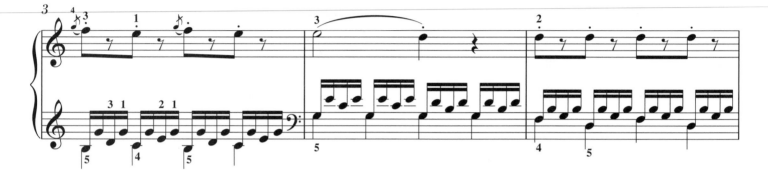

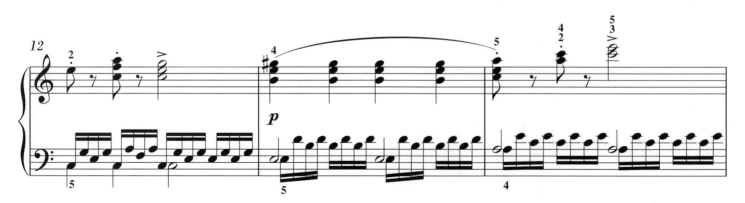

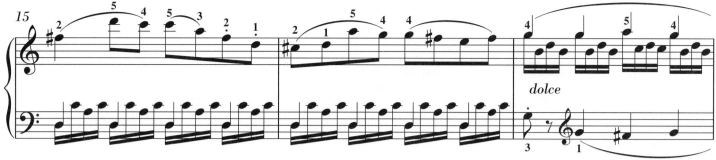

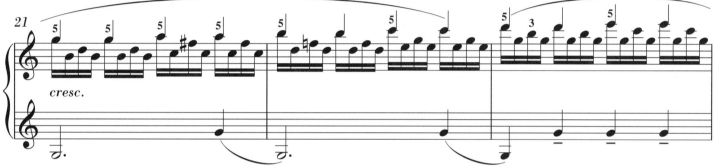

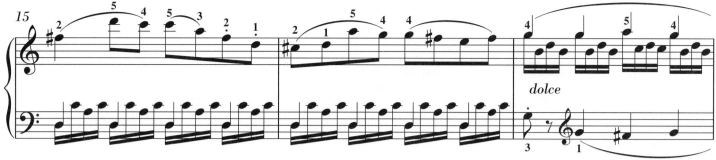

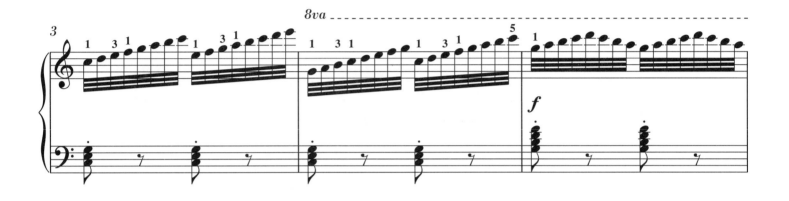

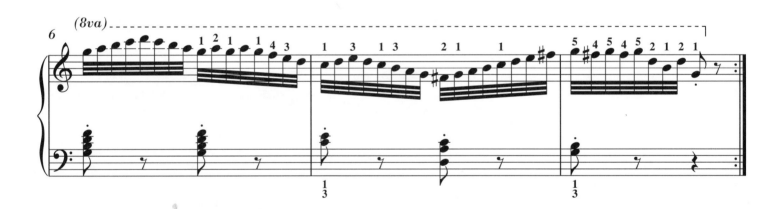

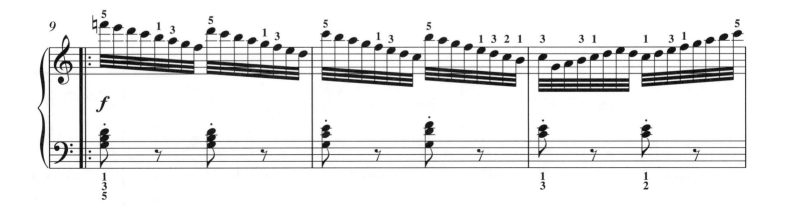

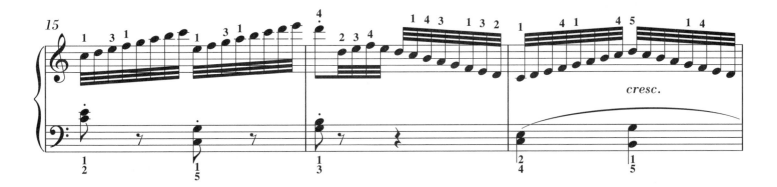

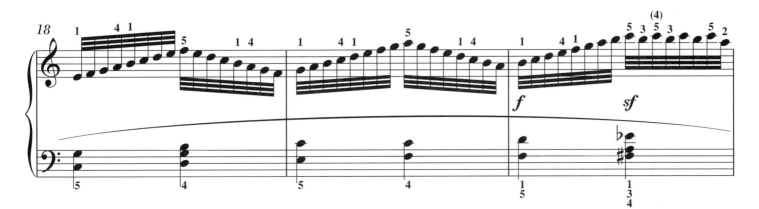

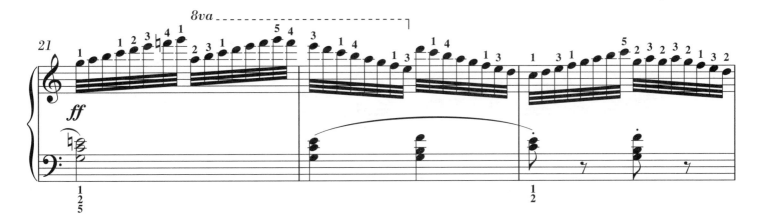

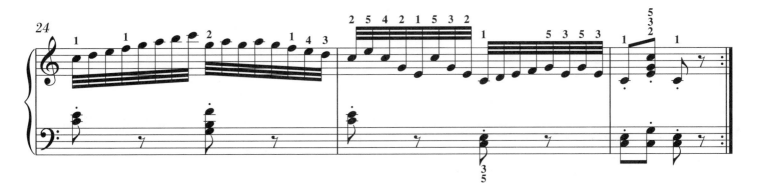

Allegretto vivace

9.

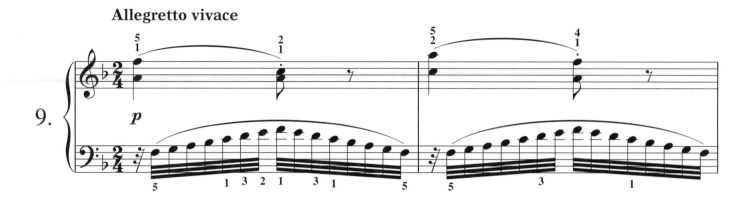

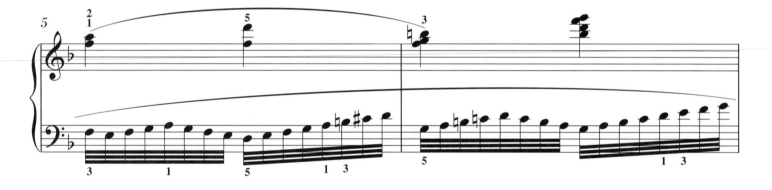

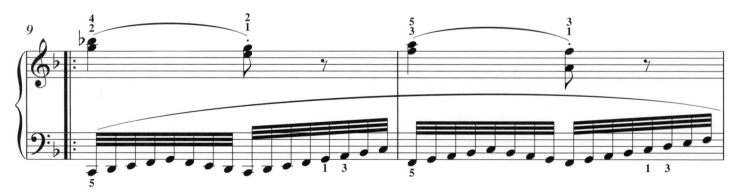

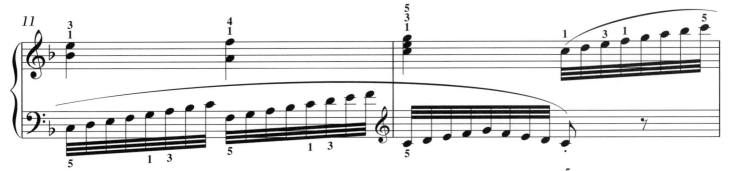

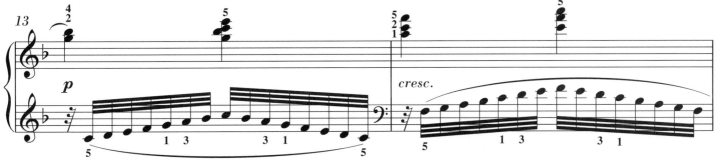

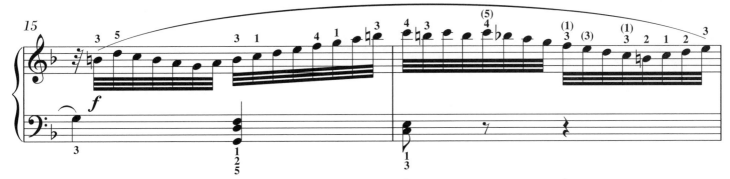

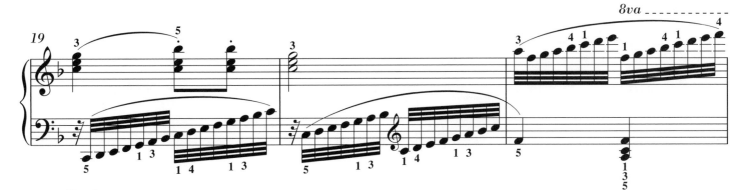

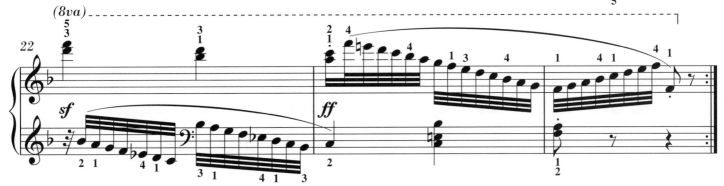

Allegro moderato

10.

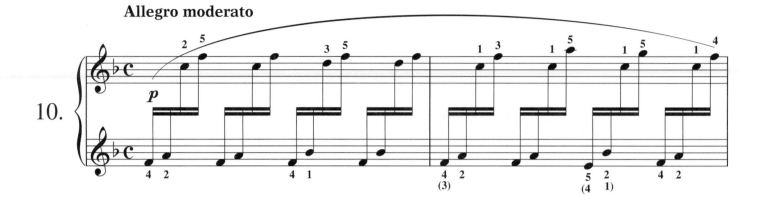

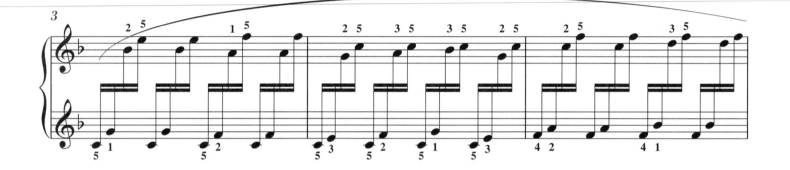

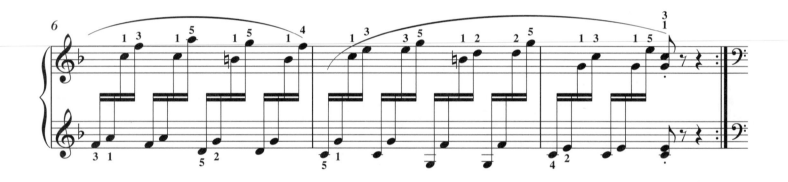

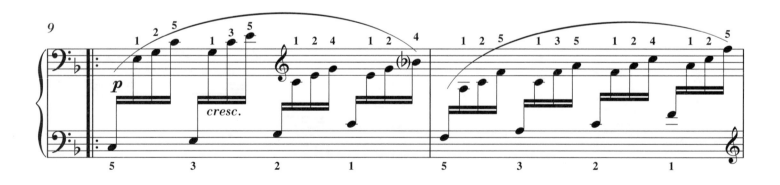

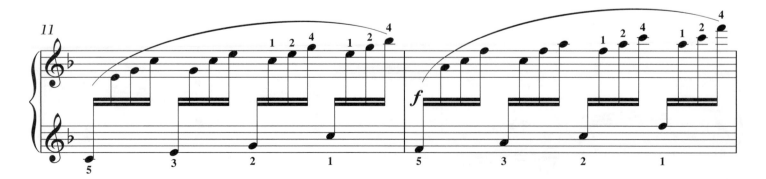

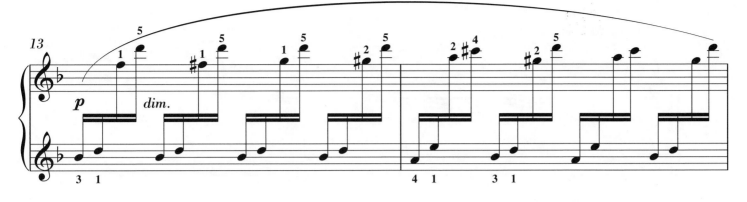

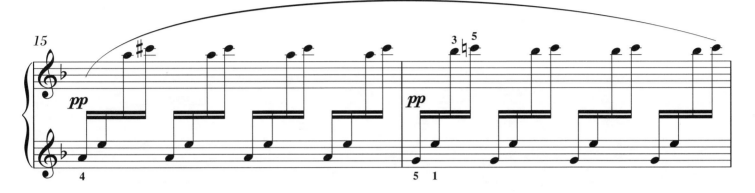

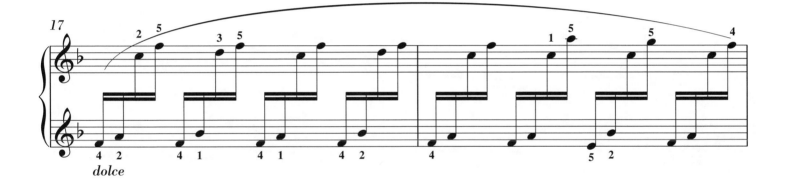

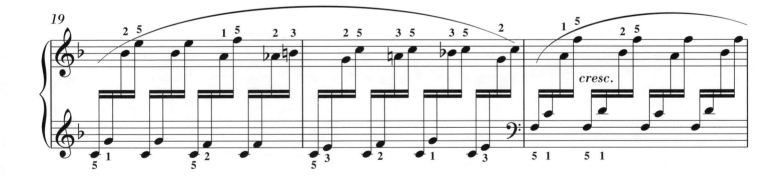

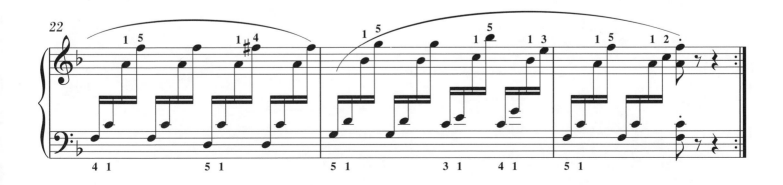

Molto vivace

11.

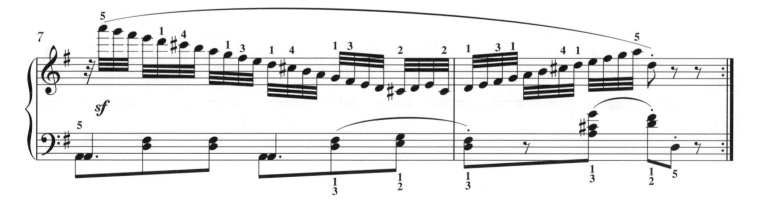

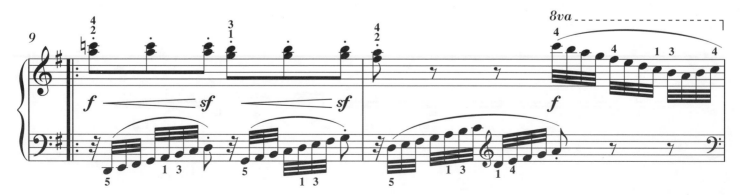

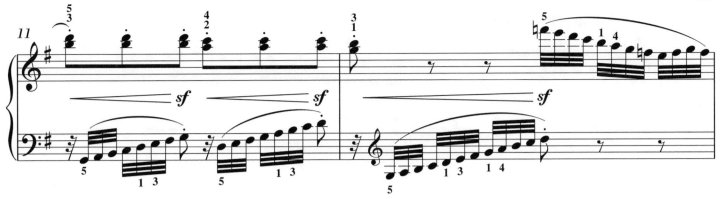

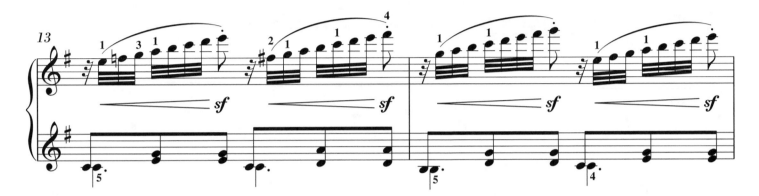

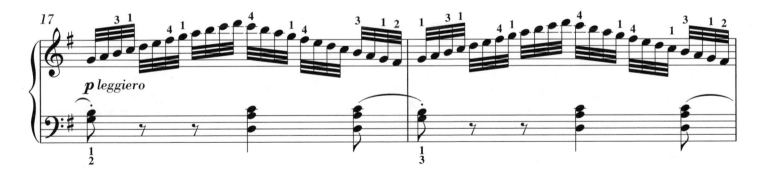

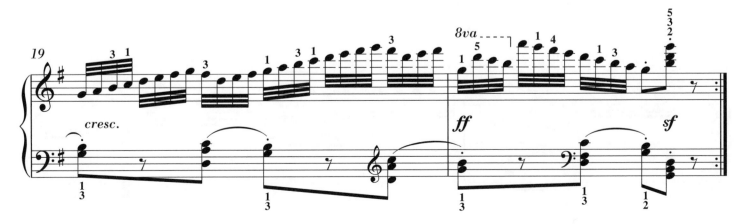

Allegretto animato

12.

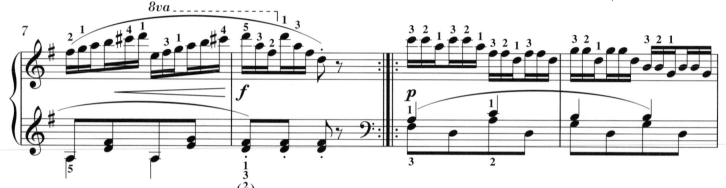

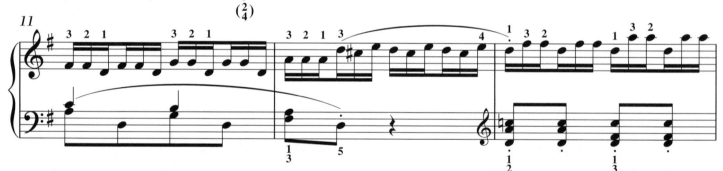

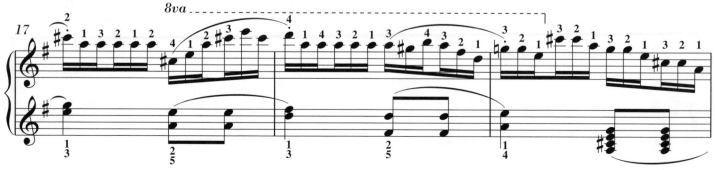

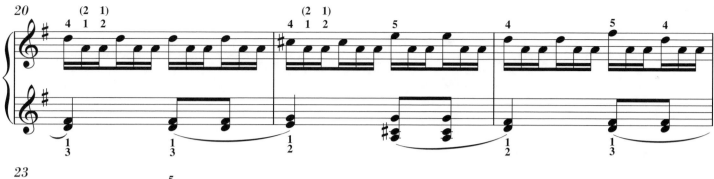

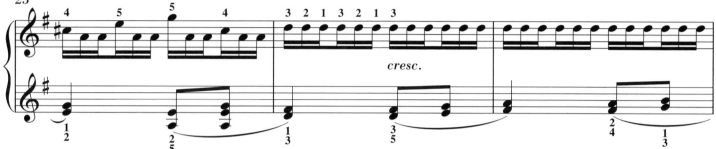

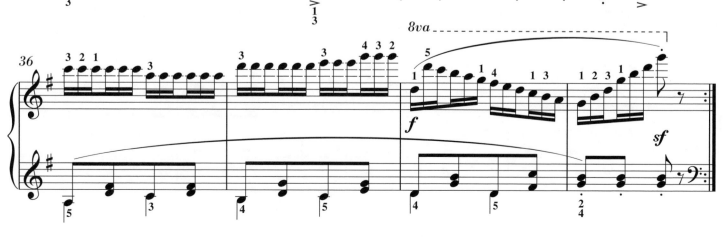

Molto vivace e leggiero

13.

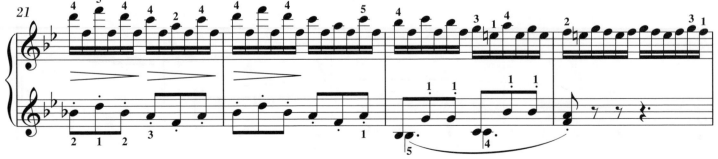

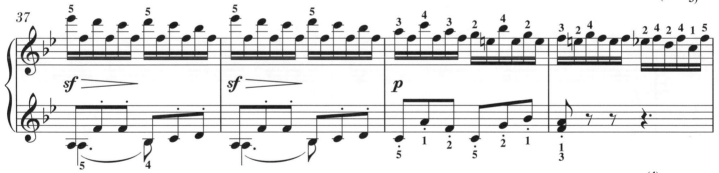

Molto vivace

14.

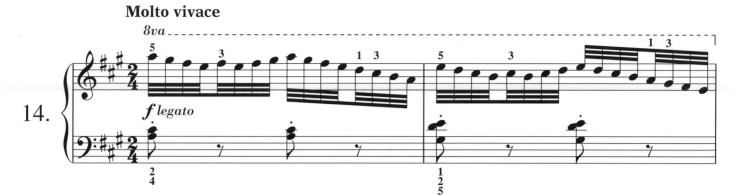

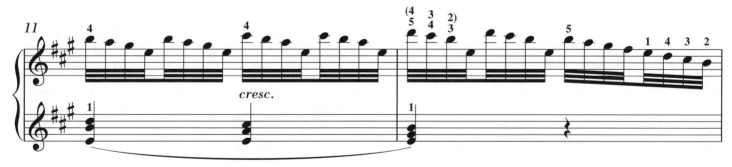

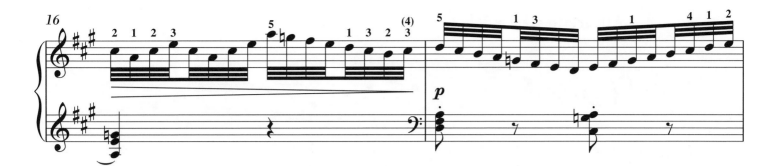

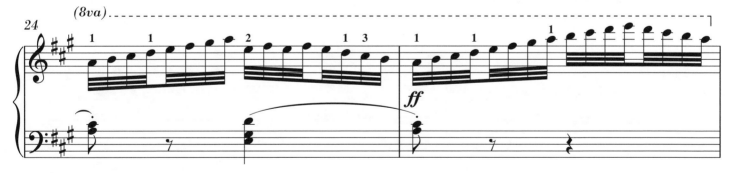

Allegretto vivace

15.

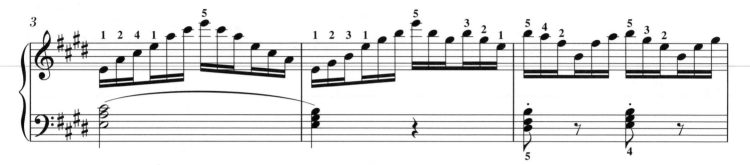

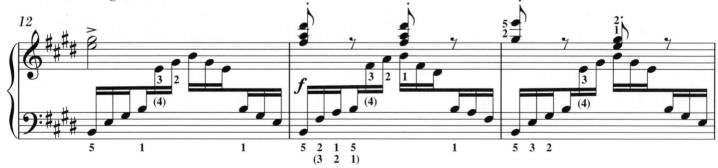

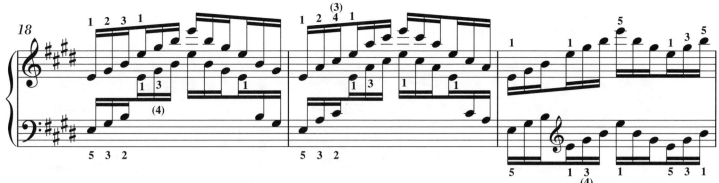

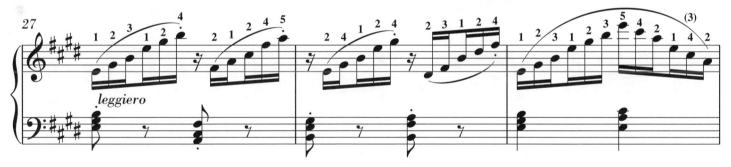

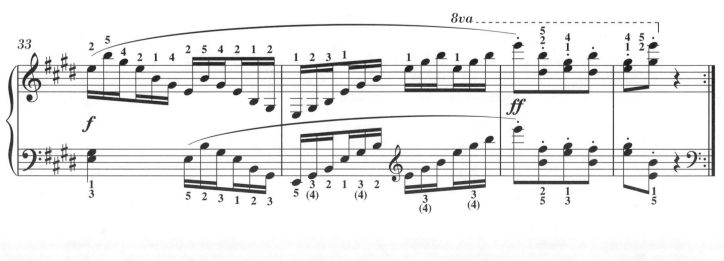

Molto vivace energico

16.

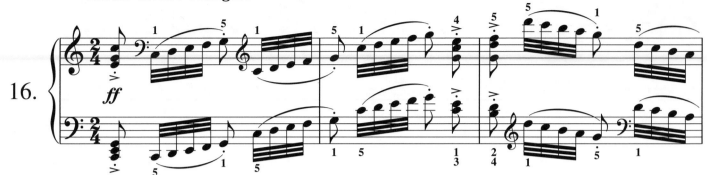

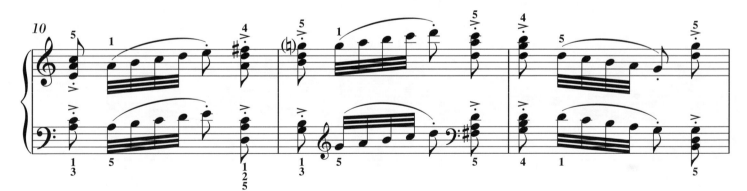

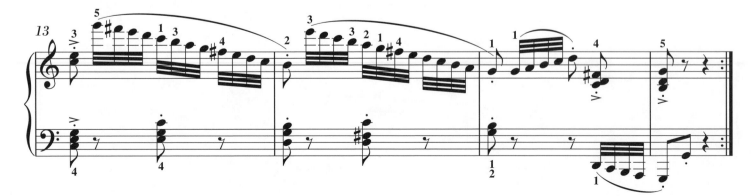

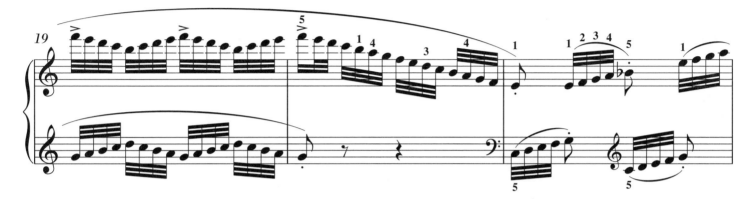

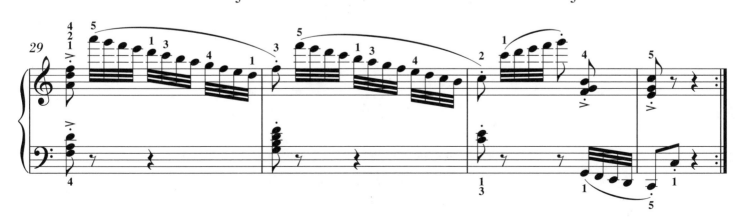

Vivace giocoso

17.

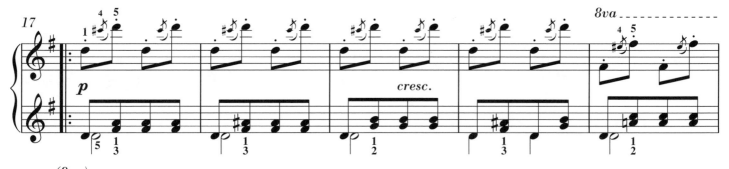

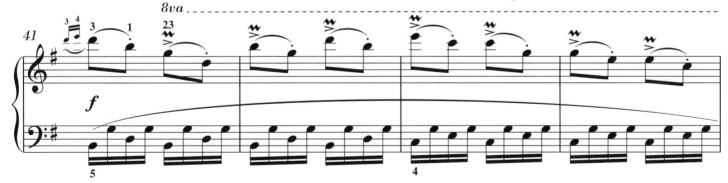

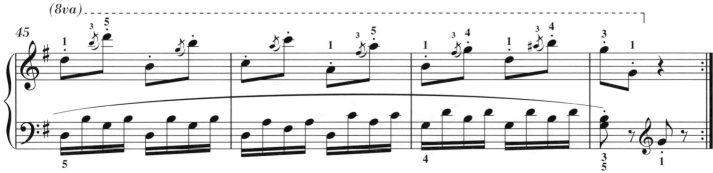

Allegro risoluto

18.

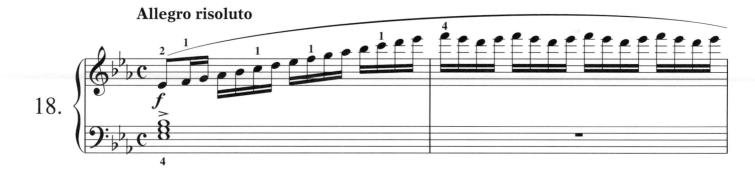

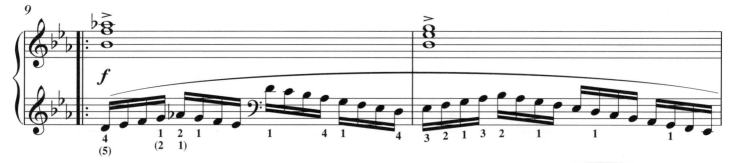

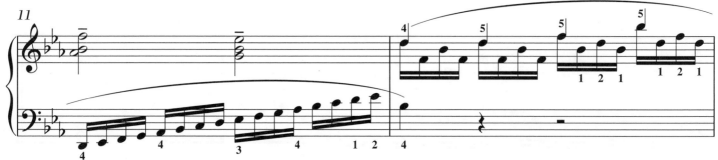

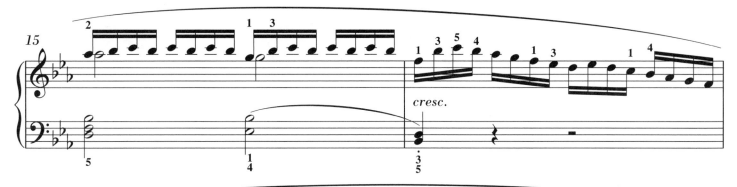

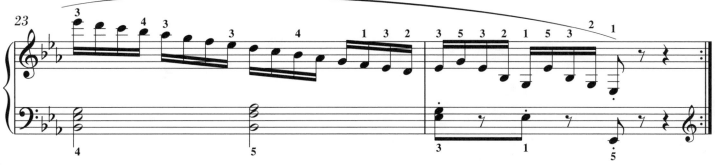

Allegro scherzando

19.

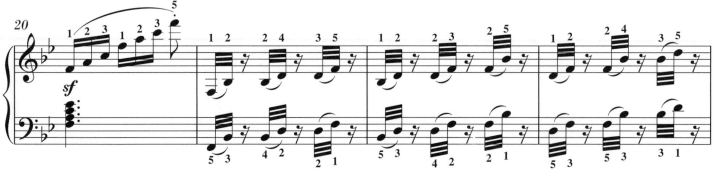

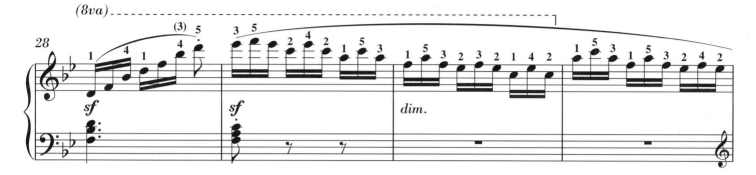

Allegro piacevole

20.

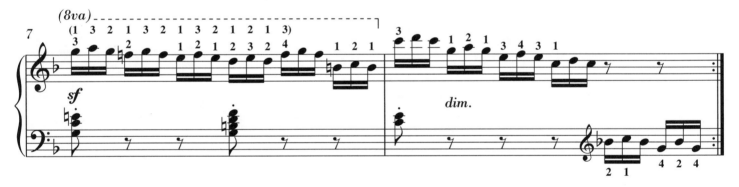

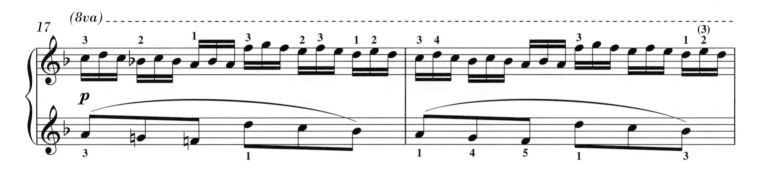

Allegro vivo

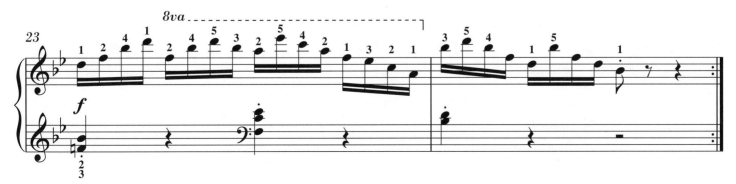

22.

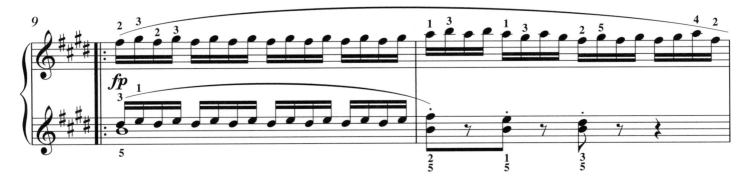

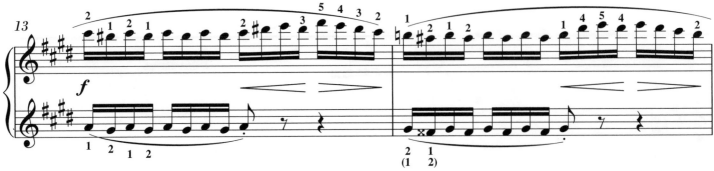

Allegro comodo

23.

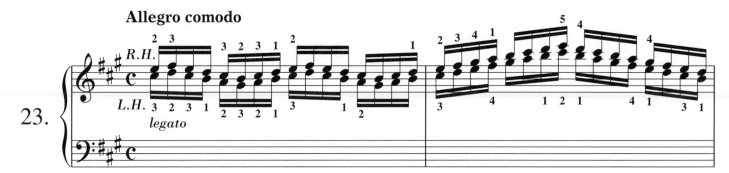

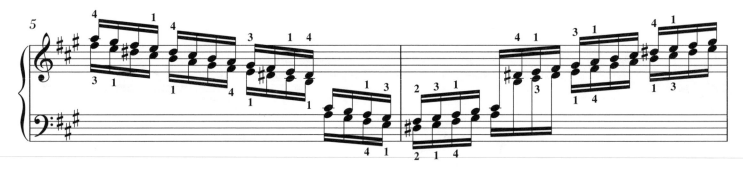

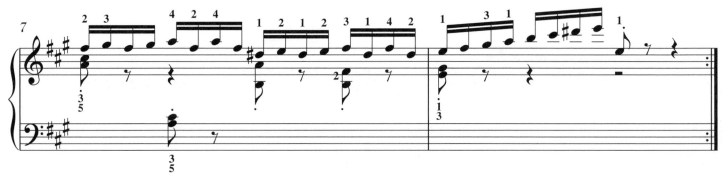

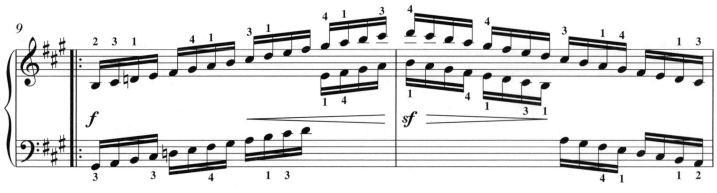

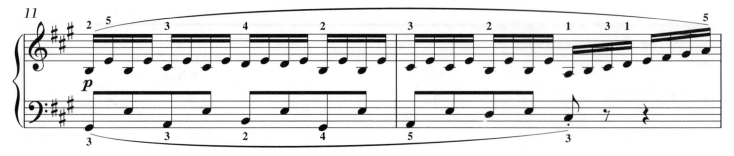

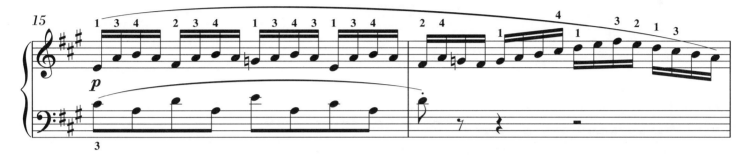

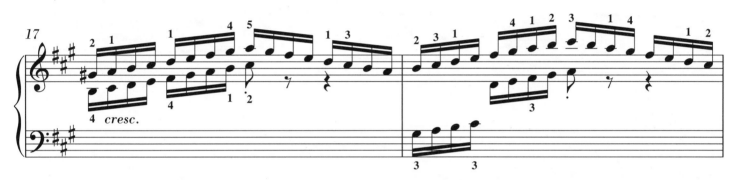

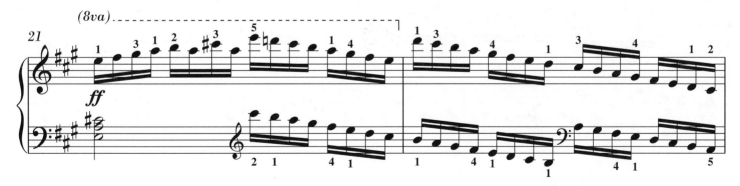

Allegro moderato

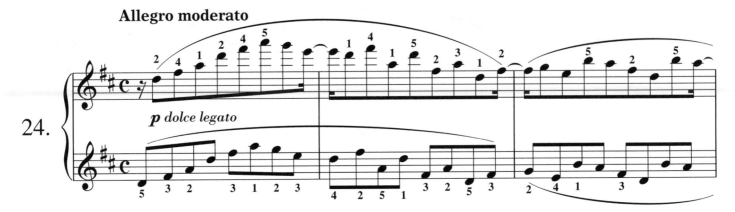

24.

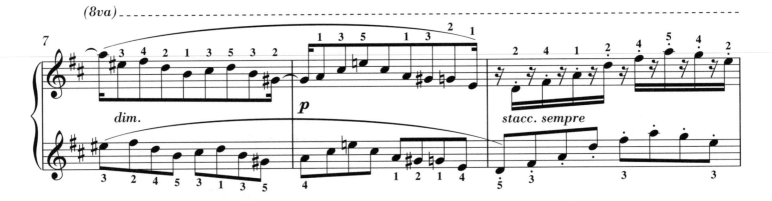

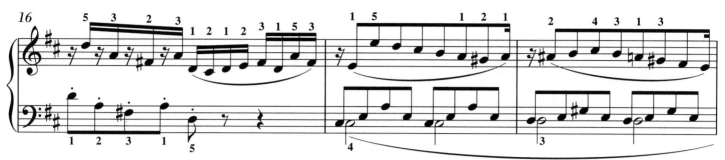

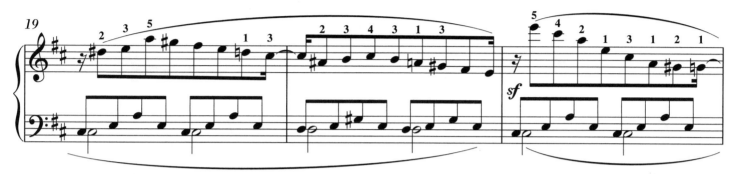

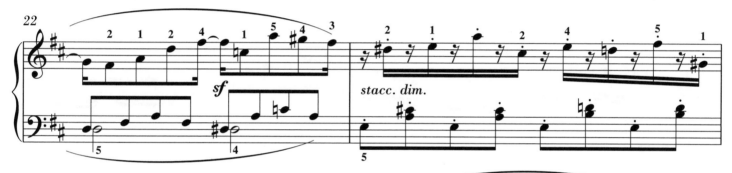

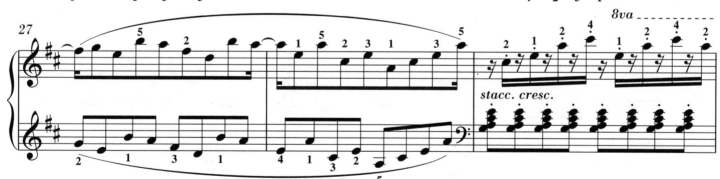

Allegro en galop

25.

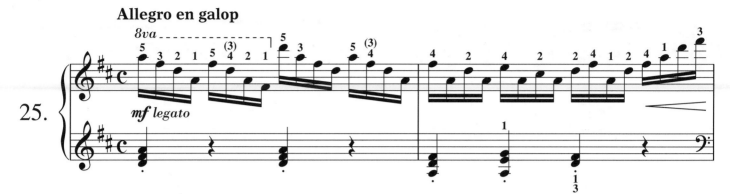

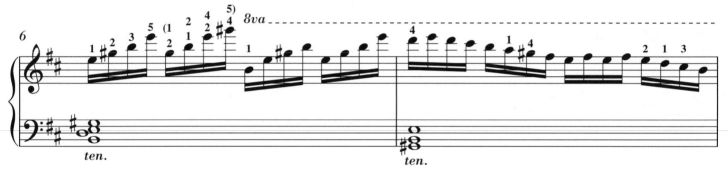

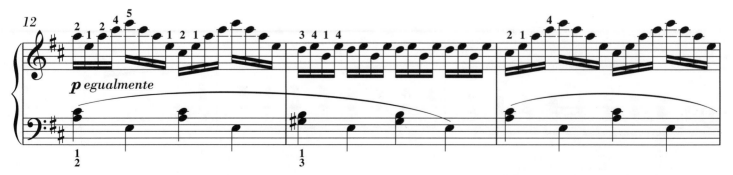

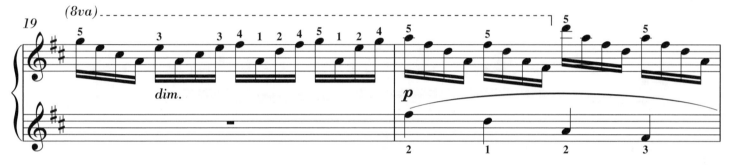

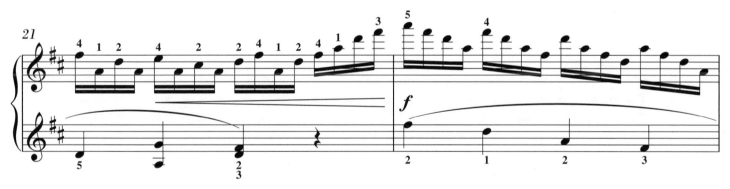

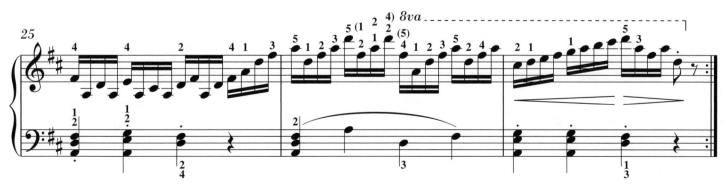

Allegretto vivace

26.

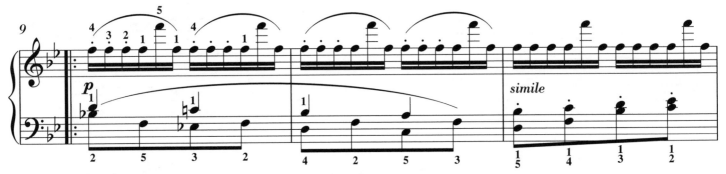

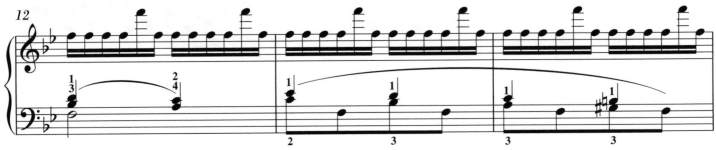

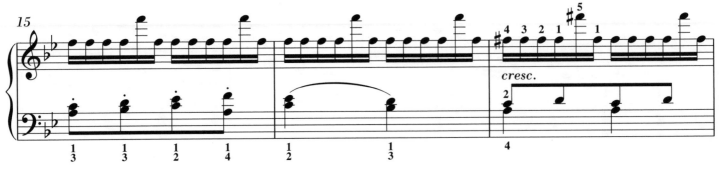

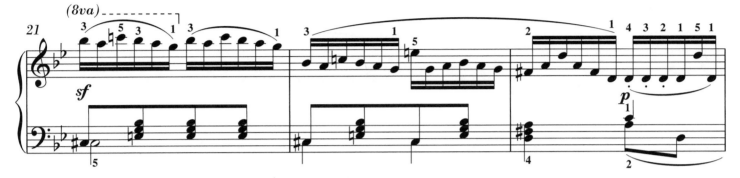

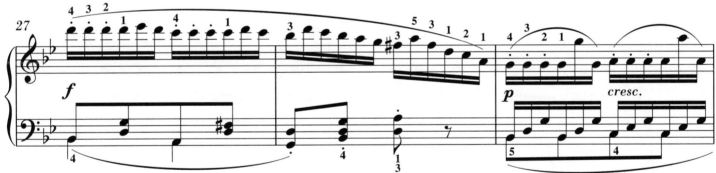

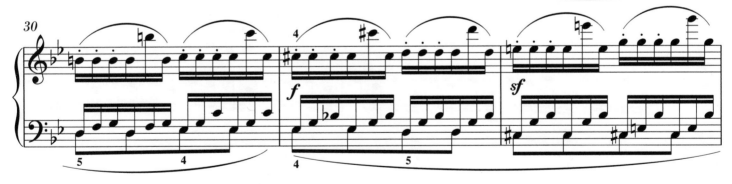

Allegro comodo

27.

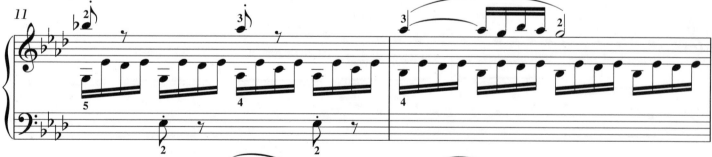

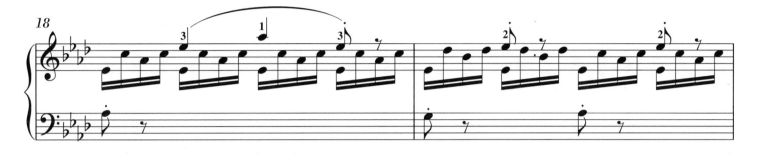

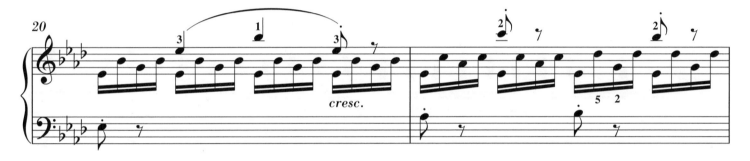

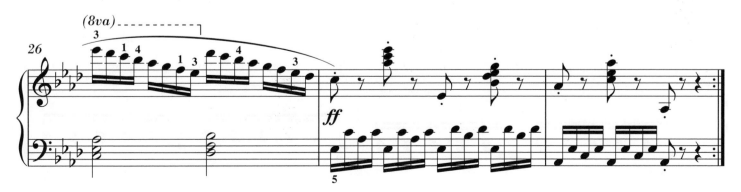

Allegro

28.

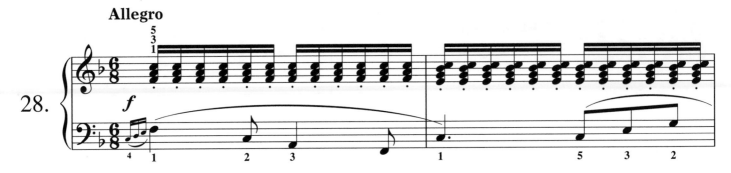

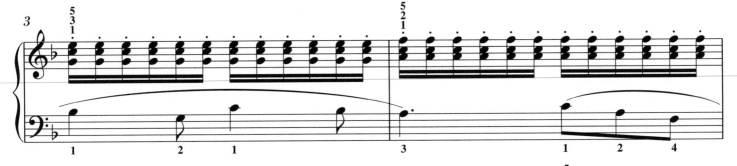

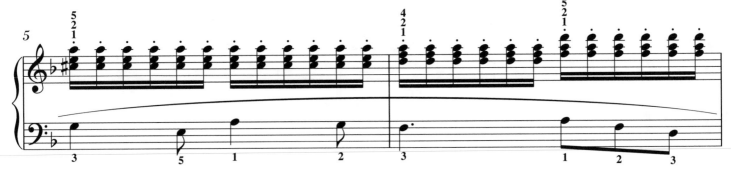

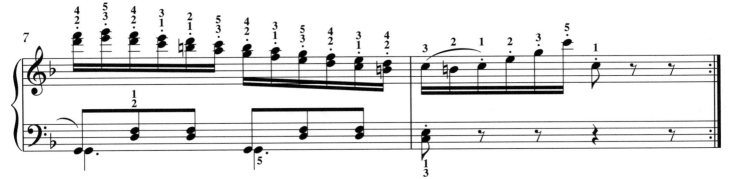

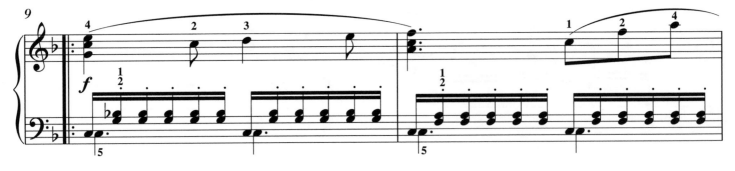

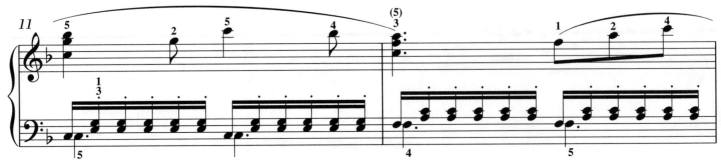

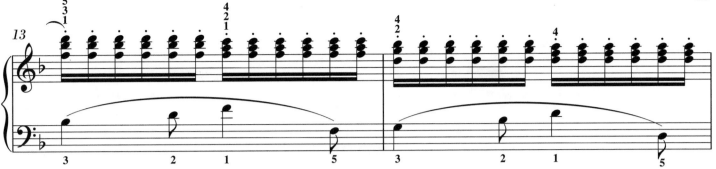

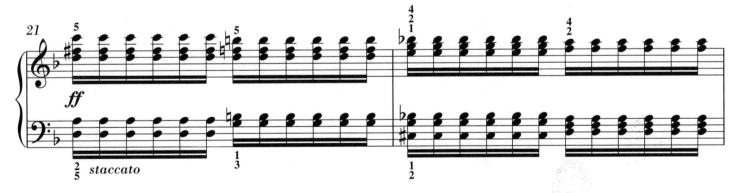

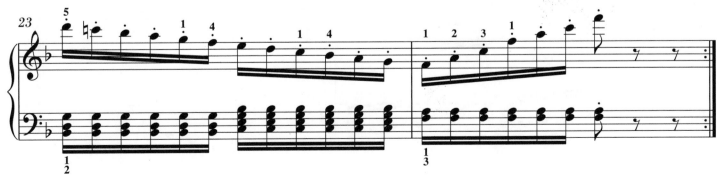

Allegro molto

29.

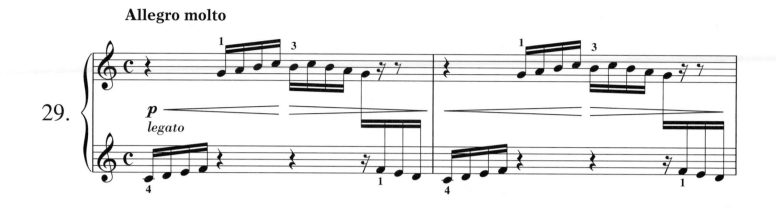

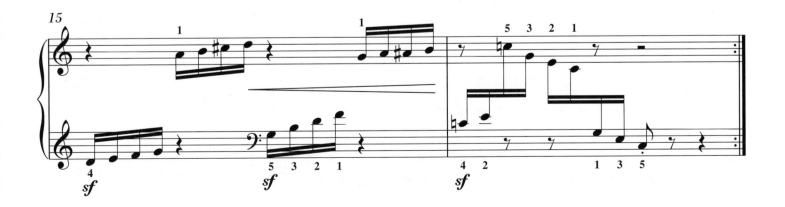

Molto vivace

30.

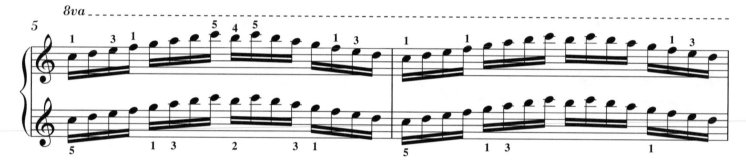

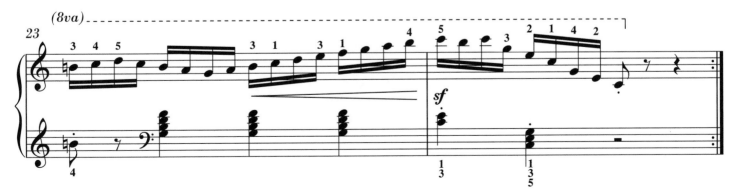

ABOUT THE EDITOR

Matthew Edwards

Dr. T. Matthew Edwards is a musician of many facets. As a pianist, he has been hailed by critics for his "...considerable talent...honest musicianship, and a formidable technique." His performances have taken him throughout the United States and to Asia, appearing as recitalist, guest artist, concerto soloist, and collaborative artist. His competition winnings include the Grand Prize in the Stravinsky Awards International Competition, and First Prize in the Music Teachers National Association National Collegiate Finals. He has previously served as part-time faculty at several colleges, including the Peabody Conservatory of Music in Baltimore, and full-time as Assistant Professor of Music at Anne Arundel Community College (AACC) in Maryland. Currently, he is Associate Professor of Music and Director of Keyboard Studies at Missouri Western State University. As a lecturer, he has been featured at the National Conference of the Music Teachers National Association, the World Piano Pedagogy Conference, and at the state conventions of the Maryland, Missouri, and Texas Music Teacher's Association. He also serves on the editorial committee for American Music Teacher magazine. As a composer, he has had major works premiered in Chicago, Salt Lake City, and the Baltimore area, and is a contributing author for the Hal Leonard Student Piano Library. As a conductor and coach, Dr. Edwards has served as the rehearsal pianist/coach for the Annapolis Opera, and musical director for Opera AACC. He lives in Kansas City, Missouri with his wife, Kelly, and their three children, Audrey, Jackson, and Cole.

www.thomasmatthewedwards.com